NEVER
Expire

Beth Stewart

Foreword by Darlene Bishop

Endorsements for

Dreams NEVER Expire

"*Dreams NEVER Expire* is one of the most inspiring books I've seen on this topic."
Darlene Bishop, Senior pastor of Solid Rock Church and founder of Darlene Bishop Ministries

"Very inspiring! *Dreams NEVER Expire* will reignite passion for broken or abandoned dreams."
Jennifer Minigh, PhD, Owner and Executive Director, ShadeTree Publishing

"Don't let your dreams get left behind! Use this book to get back on track with your destiny. *Dreams NEVER Expire* is an inspiring read that you can pretty much open to any page and be reminded of God's plan for each of us."
Paul Lalonde, Producer/Writer of *Left Behind*

"This amazing book reaches into the ancient characters of the Bible and brings a fresh relevance to everyday living. Faith explodes, hope is restored, and the love of God is experienced."
Tommy Bates, Community Family Church, Independence, K.y.

"I am excited about anyone who uses their gifts, talents, and abilities to bless the Kingdom of God. But Beth Stewart is at another level. Her humility and sensitivity to God's timing is very inspirational. This book will empower you, educate you, and give you just what you need to go to the next level in your life and ministry.
Carl Behanan, Station Manager, Christian Broadcasting System, Ltd.

"Beth's contagious passion will inspire you to arise and move boldly into your destiny – today!"
Terri Meredith, Terri Meredith Ministries

"Beth delivers a powerful truth regarding the dreams that God places within the hearts of each of us. *Dreams NEVER Expire* is power-packed with revelation that every Christian needs to know."
Sheila Salisbury-Sizemore, Instructor, Christian Healing Certification Program, Global Awakening

"I love this book. Beth's words will leave you feeling encouraged, but most of all, will challenge you to trust God and never give up on your dreams."
Brooke Griffin, CEO/founder of Skinny Mom and Cincinnati Woman of the Year

BethStewartMinistries.com

DREAMS NEVER EXPIRE

Beth Stewart
Foreword by Darlene Bishop
Copyright @ 2014 Beth Stewart Ministries
Print ISBN: 978-0-9909447-0-6
e-Book ISBN: 978-0-9909447-1-3

Scripture quotations marked NIV are taken from the HOLY BIBLE, NEW INTERNATIONAL VERSION®. Copyright © 1973, 1978, 1984 International Bible Society. Used by permission of Zondervan. All rights reserved.

Scripture quotations marked NKJV are taken from the New King James Version®. Copyright © 1982 by Thomas Nelson, Inc. All rights reserved.

Scripture quotations marked KJV are taken from the King James Version. The KJV is public domain in the United States.

Scripture taken from *The Message*. Copyright @ 1993, 1994, 1995, 1996, 2000, 2001, 2002. Used by permission of NavPress Publishing Group. All rights reserved

Scripture quotations marked AMP are taken from the Amplified® Bible, Copyright © 1954, 1958, 1962, 1964, 1965, 1987 by The Lockman Foundation. Used by permission. (www.Lockman.org)

Scripture quotations marked NLT are taken from the Holy Bible, New Living Translation copyright © 1996, 2004, 2007, 2013 by Tyndale House Foundation. Used by permission of Tyndale House Publishers Inc., Carol Stream, Illinois 60188. All rights reserved.

Photography by Heather May Photography and peshkova.

All rights reserved. This book is protected by copyright. No part of this book may be reproduced or transmitted in any form or by any means, electronic or mechanical, including photocopying, recording, or by any information storage and retrieval system, without permission in writing from the publisher.

The purpose of this book is to educate and enlighten. This book is sold with the understanding that the author and publisher are not engaged in rendering counseling, albeit it professional or lay, to the reader or anyone else. The author and publisher shall have neither liability nor responsibility to any person or entity with respect to any loss or damage caused, or alleged to have been caused, directly or indirectly, by the information contained in this book.

Visit our Web site at BethStewartMinistries.com.

My mother suggested I write a book, and even though she didn't have the opportunity to see it come to pass before she died, I would like to honor her for encouraging me and believing in me. This is for you, Mom.

Contents

Foreword by Darlene Bishop 1
Preface 5
Dreams Never Expire 7
Abraham Finally Made It, and So Can You 11
    The Waiting Game 15
    No Take Backs 18
    God Can Bless Your Mess 19
    Doubt, Be Gone 21
Joseph Fulfills His Dream, and You Will, Too 25
    It's Not Bait and Switch 27
    Life Is Not the Pits 28
    Dream Killers 35
    There Is Always Hope 37
Nehemiah Picked Up the Pieces, and So Can You ... 41
    Get a Plan 43
    Start Small, Go Big 46
    There's No "I" in *Team* 50
    The Fear Factor 53
    Nothing Is Impossible With God 56
    Squirrel!! 58
    Keep On Keeping On 62

LIVE YOUR DREAM 67
Your Heart's Desire 67
See It Happen 69
Put It on Paper 72
Put It into Prayer and Proclamation 74
Put Your Hands to Work 76
YOU CAN DO IT! 81
ABOUT THE AUTHOR 85
ABOUT BETH STEWART MINISTRIES 87
AUTHOR'S ACKNOWLEDGMENTS 88
REVIEW REQUEST 89
SCRIPTURES AND REFERENCES 91

FOREWORD
BY DARLENE BISHOP

Have you ever had a dream? Have you ever wondered how you would accomplish such a large task or even wondered whether it was possible at all? Some of us even begin to question whether God really gave us a dream after all.

Beth Stewart addresses those questions in one of the most inspiring books I've seen on this topic, *Dreams NEVER Expire*. In these pages, she addresses the challenges that most of us have faced at some point in our lives. She assures us that anyone who has ever had a God-given dream has faced challenges and obstacles to try to stop the vision from coming to pass. Beth shows us examples all through the Bible of men and women who had a dream and what circumstances they had to overcome to see it actually come to pass.

I have always said that Satan is too skilled a pirate to attack an empty ship. If God has given you a dream and you are facing trials, obstacles, fears, persecutions, time limitations, or impossible situations, you are not alone! Anyone who has fulfilled their dream has faced them as well. Just as God sees what is inside you, Satan sees it too, and he's not going to let you succeed without a fight.

We know that nothing is impossible with God. So be encouraged as you read the words on these pages. Allow this book to minister to you and speak life back into your dream. Don't let fear keep you in the boat. Step out onto the water and keep your eyes on Jesus. He will cause you to rise above everything that would defeat you. Dream so big that if God's not in it, the fulfillment will be impossible. It's time to stop letting anything hold you back.

Remember, Dreams NEVER Expire!

About Darlene Bishop Ministries

Darlene Bishop Ministries (DarleneBishop.org) is an outreach of Solid Rock Church, in Monroe, Ohio, where Darlene shares pastoral duties with her son,

Lawrence Bishop II. Darlene began preaching in 1984 at local women's meetings and in her home church, but her ministry began to expand nationally in 1998. Darlene Bishop Ministries is now traveling full time, and she appears regularly on international Christian television programs. This ministry was established to reach the lost, the broken, and the hurting–to reveal that victory can be obtained every time, if you only BELIEVE.

The compassion Darlene has is shown through the various ministries that she has founded and supports, such as the Home for Life and the Brazilian Orphanage. Darlene Bishop Ministries is spreading the gospel across the nation and around the world.

Dreams NEVER Expire

PREFACE

This book was written for those who desire to become all that God designed them to be. It is for those who dare to dream and walk out their divine assignment.

As you read this book, it is my desire that you will search your heart and reignite the passion for your dreams. It is designed to help you understand that, no matter how much time has passed or what has happened in your life, it is never too late to fulfill your dreams and to walk along your divine path. I hope you will be encouraged to dream again and take a step of faith to fulfill your purpose.

I pray that wisdom and revelation will come to you, that the eyes of your understanding will be opened, and that you may know the hope of God's purpose in your life and how He has set aside a rich and glorious inheritance for you to accomplish it.

Dreams NEVER Expire

DREAMS NEVER EXPIRE

Have you ever wondered whether you missed out on life because you waited too long? Maybe you had a dream or a vision for your life and didn't have the time or resources to fulfill it. I have good news for you. It's never too late to fulfill your dreams and walk in the fullness of God's purpose for your life.

There are many instances in the Bible when men and women were well up in age before their dreams were finally achieved. Consider Abraham and Sarah. God promised Abraham that he would have a son and would go on to become the father of many nations. God first gave Abraham and his wife, Sarah, this promise when they had no children, and then continued to reinstate the promise throughout the years.[1] I am sure their doubts multiplied as they grew older each year with no evidence of the vow in sight. Abraham's frustration shows that he was very much human just like the rest of us and that, no matter how impossible things may appear in our life, if we just hang in there and be persistent, we will see our promise come to pass just like Abraham's. Eventually, Abraham had the promised son and later he became known as father of many nations. If Abraham could finally make it, then you can, too!

Like Abraham, Joseph was given a promise for his future and faced many obstacles before he saw it come to fruition. When he was a young man, Joseph dreamed about his role in his family. The brothers knew the dreams meant that Joseph, whom they already resented because their father favored him so much, would one day rule over them. In an attempt to thwart the destiny, they initiated a chain of events in Joseph's life that would carry him in a direction opposite from what the dream showed. Nevertheless, Joseph remained faithful to God, and the promise could not be denied. If Joseph's dream could still be fulfilled, then yours can, too!

Nehemiah faced a seemingly impossible dream to rebuild the city of Jerusalem. He didn't let death threats or distractions sway him from his purpose, though. Instead, he made a plan, rolled up his sleeves, got to work, and rebuilt the city walls in only fifty-two days. If Nehemiah could pick up the shattered pieces of his dream and make it happen, then you can, too!

Many people relinquish their dreams to things such as impatience, deception, doubt, and shame. We must make up our minds that God is faithful and believe that God will come through for us. Instead of blaming God when we don't see our dreams coming to pass, we should trust Him and take Him at His Word, which says that *"God is not a human being that He should lie, not a human being that He should change His mind. Does He speak and then not act? Does He promise and not fulfill?"*[2]

It doesn't matter what you've been through or how long you have waited. If you persevere with your faith and are determined, you will see your promise come to fruition.

This book uses the personal stories of Abraham, Joseph, Nehemiah, and myself to prove and illustrate that dreams never expire.

Dreams NEVER Expire

Dream Again

What promises and / or dreams are you holding on to?

What promises and / or dreams have you let go?

ABRAHAM FINALLY MADE IT, AND SO CAN YOU

One day when Abraham was seventy-five years old, the Lord commanded him to leave his country and travel to a promised land. The Lord promised to make Abraham and his offspring into a great nation, and declared that his name would be great and that he and all the families of the earth would be blessed.[3] Abraham immediately departed with Sarah, his wife; Lot, his brother's son; and all their possessions.

Over the next ten years, the Lord continued to tell Abraham that his descendants would be innumerable; however, Abraham and Sarah never saw fruition of the promise and became disheartened. They took things into their own hands, and Abraham conceived a child with Sarah's Egyptian maidservant, Hagar.[4] When Abraham was eighty-six years old, Ishmael was born.

Dreams NEVER Expire

Later, when Abraham was in his upper nineties, the Lord appeared to him again and told him that he and Sarah would soon have a baby boy.[5] Abraham fell on his face, laughed, and questioned how a hundred-year-old man and a ninety-year-old woman could pull this off.[6] Sarah laughed, too, and wondered how it could be.[7] Despite their concerns, their promised son, Isaac, was born.

Despite all the turns and twists in Abraham's life, he eventually saw the son God had promised. He never did, though, personally see the multitudes of nations that were birthed from his heritage because they are still living on today.

When God gives us a dream, we all have the same temptations to either quit or find another way to make it happen. The story of Abraham teaches us that Abraham tried to solve his own problem because he became impatient when Sarah didn't conceive a child in his anticipated timing. He took his wife's servant and had a child with her instead. (This was an accepted practice in ancient times.) It is important to note here that Sarah had a major influence on Abraham's decision to conceive a child with Hagar.

Abraham sometimes takes a lot of bad rap for this problem, but Sarah is to blame, as well. It was actually her idea in the first place.[8]

The birth and life of Abraham and Hagar's child, Ishmael, only made Sarah jealous that she didn't have her own son, and it quickly resulted in dissension in Abraham's family. This family dysfunction could have been avoided had Abraham and Sarah just been a little more patient. This story sounds like many of ours today. We are still seeing the results of rash mistakes made in our past.

I've had to learn to trust God in my life just like everyone else. After I graduated college, I set out to my "promised land," like Abraham, only my Canaan was a full-time teaching job in a small town in eastern Kentucky, where I knew God wanted me to be. The school was one of the top schools in the state, and there was a long list of applicants vying for positions that rarely opened because teachers who were lucky enough to be hired in this school district never left. Many teachers continued working well into their sixties.

It did not look promising for me to get a job, and people surrounded me with seeds of doubt. I could have given up like so many others and gone to other school districts less desirable and farther away. Instead, I kept declaring the promises of God and maintained my belief that He would answer my prayers. When the doubts threatened a coup on my faith, I would get right back on track.

After less than a year of substitute teaching, I landed a full-time permanent position teaching fourth grade. I probably was not the most qualified applicant or the one who had been waiting the longest, but I believe it was the favor of God in my life. He had been working on my behalf to fulfill His promises. If He would do this for me, then He will do it for you, too.

My first classroom of students.

The Waiting Game

The year-after-year wait for a child began to weigh on Abraham's faith. He eventually expressed his honest concerns to God. He said, *"Sovereign Lord, what can you give me since I remain childless and the one who will inherit my estate is Eliezer of Damascus? You have given me no children; so a servant in my household will be my heir."*⁹

The waiting game is what Abraham had to deal with, and what we have to deal with, as well. In today's society, instant gratification is the most prevalent drug, and we look to time-management experts to teach us how to find ways to produce more in less time. Because we cannot tolerate the idea of waiting, we find ways to fill the void with immediate mini-accomplishments to make us feel like we are getting closer to our answer. One of the hot buzzwords in the current corporate generation is *low-hanging fruit*, which refers to something that can be easily reached with minimal effort.

We all struggle with wanting to see the fruit of our dreams coming to life and ripening. It doesn't help that we are encouraged to "actively wait," which in a nutshell means to reach for other things associated with the dream while we wait. At first glance, active waiting looks much more appealing than passive waiting, which is us doing much of nothing while we sulk and give ourselves over to disappointment. However, the intention behind active waiting may become twisted, and we may find ourselves grasping at straws to make anything that resembles the dream occur. In the case of Abraham, he was very active during his waiting time, but his activity in the bed of another woman was his part of the plan, not God's.

If God had a list of suggested activities for active waiting, it would look more like the following:

* keeping the Lord's ways (Psalm 37:34)
* hoping in the Word (Psalm 130:5)
* remaining quiet; not complaining (Lamentations 3:26)
* continuing in prayer and supplication (Acts 1:14)
* staying eager and persevering (Romans 8:25)
* listening and watching for the Lord (Proverbs 8:34)
* reminding oneself to wait continually (Hosea 12:6)
* seeking first His kingdom and His righteousness (Matthew 6:33)

I once knew a young girl who was believing God for her ideal husband. Although she dated several fine young men, she never found any of them to be "the one." Several years passed, and she became weary, began to doubt, and started compromising the characteristics that, for her, would make up an ideal husband. After resolving that her standards were too high and determining that she needed to be more realistic, she eventually agreed to marry a man who was far from her previous expectations and even further from the Lord. Not long after the wedding, I watched her passion for the Lord slowly fade and her marriage fall into ruin.

So many people are like this woman—and Abraham's wife, Sarah—who got tired of waiting and settled for less. Waiting is never easy, and waiting particularly on God to act in our lives may be the hardest task we will ever face. Although Abraham and Sarah struggled with their faith like we do, they were still able to witness all that God had promised them.

We must be careful when playing the waiting game of life because it has always been a trick of the enemy to sow doubt and confusion in our minds concerning the promises of God, and if he wins, we lose.

No Take Backs

God chose us before the foundation of the world.[10] Numbers 23:19 reminds us that God does not lie, nor does He change His mind; if He said it, He will do it. The Lord knew us (what gifts and talents we would be born with) even before He formed us in our mothers' wombs.[11] The Bible says that His gifts and callings are without repentance.[12] I particularly like the way the Message Bible says it: *"God's gifts and God's call are under full warranty—never canceled, never rescinded."* Whatever God put inside of us when He created us, He is never going to change His mind or take it back. Personally, however, I do believe gifts are not fully available for people living in sin, but when they get on the right path with God, the gifts will begin to operate in their life as He has designed.

It is possible to delay our promises if we continue down the wrong path, but according to the Word of God, He is not going to take the gifts back just because we are messing up. Resources may be a different story, though, according to the parable of the talents that Jesus told.[13] In the story, a master gave each of his three servants five, two, or one talent (an amount of money). Two of the servants took the money and made more. The master was pleased with them and gave them even more. The third servant buried his single talent in fear of losing it and had nothing to show when the master inquired. The master called him a wicked and slothful servant and took the talent from him and gave it to one of the other servants.

God never gives up on His people. When everyone else seems to be giving up on you, God is still with you and cheering you on until you get on the designated path for your life. Though man will fail you, God will never leave you or forsake you.[14] EVER!

God Can Bless Your Mess

In his doubt and restlessness to see God's promise fulfilled, Abraham decided to help God speed up the process by initiating action outside of God's will. Have you ever done anything like that? Have you ever tried to hurry things along to make them fit your personal timeline?

God has His own timetable for things; however, we tend to jump in and make things happen outside of His timing, and we end up birthing our own mess to take care of while we wait for our promise.

There is more good news we can glean from Abraham's story, though. God blessed everything that Abraham set his hands to, including Ishmael and Hagar. God will also bless us despite any mistakes we make, as long as we repent and commit our ways to Him. He can turn our messes around, and we can still fulfill our destinies. That is good news for us all, because everyone has messed up at some point in life. Thankfully, the Bible says that the Lord works all things together for good to those who love Him and who have been called according to His purpose.[15] I could shout hallelujah right here!

What obstacles are in your life, or what mistakes have you made that leave you feeling like there's no hope? The same promise that Abraham was given is also given to us. The Lord is calling us to walk before Him. He will multiply and bless us, if we will dare to believe.[16]

Doubt, Be Gone

The Bible refers to Abraham (whose name means "father of many") as the father of faith, because Abraham faithfully listened and obeyed God's voice and kept His commandments, His statutes, and His laws.[17] Abraham packed up his family and possessions and left his homeland to follow God to an unknown place. This is a huge commitment! Sometimes we need to ask ourselves if our heart is ready and willing to go anywhere that God tells us. If we really want to please God, then we must always remember that without faith it's impossible to please Him.[18]

Even though Abraham was the father of faith, he still had doubts and trials that followed the promise God had given him. However, when Abraham had doubts, he went to God. It's okay to be honest with God. He knows how we feel, and He wants to communicate with us about it. Be honest with Him, and remember that He is your heavenly Father and loves you. He understands. Keep in mind, though, that God will never change His Word. What He has written is written. Since His Word is immovable, then it's up to us to line up with it.

If doubts arise because we lack information or understanding about the situation, then we need to pray for wisdom. The Bible says that if we lack wisdom, we should ask of God, who gives generously to all without finding fault, and it will be given us.[19] I love how this says that wisdom *will* (not *might*) be given, and we won't be penalized for asking.

The enemy will always send people to discourage us and convince us that God is not really going to do what He promised. I call these people "unbelieving believers." They believe in God, but not in the promises He makes. The devil is a liar who comes to steal, kill, and destroy.[20] One of his greatest strategies is deception. Don't fall victim to his schemes. Instead, know that if God said it, then you can take it to the bank. Surround yourself with people who will believe with you.

Abraham did finally receive the promise, but he brought a lot of unnecessary problems on his family by listening to people of doubt. When God gives you a promise and you can back it up with the Word of God, don't let anyone talk you out of it. Your promise will come. Maybe not in your timing and probably not the way you think, but God knows what is best for you and how to bring it to pass.

Walking by total faith and putting doubt to death is not an overnight process. It generally takes many years of walking with God before we are willing to blindly venture wherever He calls. When we wait, we should seek the Lord continually and remember the wonders He has done. Sometimes when I'm believing for the impossible, I remind myself that God is the same yesterday, today, and forever. If He parted the Red Sea, then it is possible for me to be saved from my situation, as well. I remind myself of the covenant God made with Abraham and how that covenant belongs to me, too.

****

God will never give up on you, so what are you waiting for? Let go of all those excuses and start planning to fulfill that dream—you know, the dream you let go because of circumstances or mistakes. It's time to pick it back up and trust that things will be different this time.

Dreams NEVER Expire

The Lord your God will bless you in all the works of your hands. He has been watching over your journey.[21] The Bible says that the Lord shall command the blessing on you and all that you undertake.[22] Oh my goodness, that is exciting news for us believers! Aren't you glad that you can start all over, and even though you have messed up (like the rest of us), God is still going to bless you, just like He did Abraham? You'd better shout right here!

Why do you think God makes us wait sometimes?

How has God used the messes in your life for your good?

What is the biggest doubt in your mind concerning your dream, and what does God say about it?

JOSEPH FULFILLS HIS DREAM, AND YOU WILL, TOO

Joseph is known as the man of God who went from the pit to the prison and then the palace. He is a picture of patience.[23]

Joseph was one of twelve boys in his family, and son to his father's favorite wife, Rachel. His father, Israel, loved Joseph more than any of his other brothers, and he made him a fancy coat to show his affection. When Joseph's brothers saw the coat, their hatred and jealousy of Joseph burned within them.

When Joseph was a young man, he dreamed that his brothers' sheaves of grain were bowing down to his sheaves.[24] Then he had another dream that the sun, moon, and eleven stars were bowing down to him.[25] Joseph told his brothers the dreams, and they hated him all the more because they knew the dreams meant that Joseph, whom they already resented, would one day rule over them. They set into motion a plan to thwart Joseph's destiny.

While pasturing their father's sheep in a distant field, the brothers saw Joseph approaching from afar and began to create a plan for his demise. Once he approached, they tossed him into a pit, and later sold him as a slave to a passing caravan. This situation certainly did not resemble the dream Joseph had. In fact, it began to look impossible for the dream to come to pass.

Sadly, Joseph's story gets worse before it ever gets better. He was sold again to Potiphar (one of Pharaoh's officials and the captain of his guard). With humility and hard work, Joseph rose to a position of overseer of Potiphar's estate, only to be cast into the prison due to false accusations by Potiphar's wife.

Through a series of God-ordained events, Joseph rose once again and was placed in charge of Pharaoh's palace. He was second in command and only answered to Pharaoh. With Joseph's great wisdom and kingdom management, he was able to stockpile food and supplies to overcome a harsh famine across the region. The famine eventually brought Joseph's brothers to Egypt to buy food, where they found themselves bowing down to him just as the dreams predicted.

Despite the disparity of Joseph's situations with his dreams, he remained faithful to God and so the promise could not be denied. If Joseph could still reach his dream despite slavery and imprisonment, then we can reach ours regardless of our tough times, too.

It's Not Bait and Switch

We are no different from Joseph. As soon as God gives us a dream, here come the testing and trials. I am pretty sure that Joseph felt like a fool when his times of testing and trials came. He had a dream, but he landed in the pit, and it didn't end there. He also landed in prison and was unjustly accused of making sexual advances on Potiphar's wife.

Joseph must have felt like a victim of bait and switch. This game is a common tactic of the enemy. As soon as he sees a promise made over our lives, he comes in like a flood to kill, steal, and destroy our dreams of seeing it fulfilled.[26]

For many of us, our journey may not take us exactly where we wanted or thought we would go, but if we will hold on to our dream, just like Joseph did, then we will eventually arrive at our final destination.

In my own journey with God, many times nothing made sense. In fact, everything seemed to go the opposite of my dream and the fulfillment of my dream seemed impossible. Before I received the revelation in this book I'm sharing with you, I can remember constantly saying, "I can't see how any of these things God showed me could possibly happen." I will be very honest with you and say that many times I just wanted to give up. My only dilemma was that I had nothing better to go back to. I certainly didn't want to stay in the same place. I knew my past worldly life was empty, so I saw no alternative than to press forward in my wilderness journey.

Life Is Not the Pits

Like Joseph, every person has pit experiences in life. There are many types of pits, and we all deal with them from time to time. How we handle ourselves in the pit, however, will determine how swiftly we can get out of it. Our attitude during this time is crucial. It is important that discouragement does not trick us into taking up residence there.

Pit experiences are times of personal development and deal mostly with the *cooking* of our character. (Sometimes our pit may resemble a vat of hot water that we find ourselves in.) Think of character development in terms of a Crock-Pot versus a microwave. God tends to use a Crock-Pot approach (slow and steady) when we would prefer the microwave (fast and convenient). Everyone hates the word *patience*, but it is a fact that we must be patient while we wait. As we all know, there are no microwave character traits in the kingdom of God, and microwave faith won't do us much good.

Our heart attitude is very important to how we handle our dream when it comes. We must be ready for it. Our pit experiences have a purpose. For example, Joseph's pit experience developed humility and character because he had a big assignment to fulfill as the second in command of a nation.

When we are in a pit experience, it is tempting to build walls around ourselves and disconnect from friends, family, and even God. Instead, we need to surround ourselves with dreamers and other people who will inspire us. If you are in a pit experience, you will need encouragers, because I promise you that the enemy will send enough discouragers to try to prevent the fulfillment of your dream.

I understand what it is like to build walls. When my mother, who was my mentor and best friend, passed away, I was upset with God. I didn't believe she was old enough to die. Within months after being diagnosed with cancer, she was gone from this earth, and I was angry. When people would try to console me, I responded with all the right words, things like: "Well, God is in control." "God had a purpose for this." "You can't question God." Despite what my mouth said, my heart ached and I built spiritual walls around it for protection and hiding. I learned to smile, but inside I was inconsolable. I stopped most of my Christian fellowship activities (a very bad idea), because I didn't want to be around people. I wanted and needed time to heal.

I didn't handle my situation biblically. Even though I knew that the Bible said to not forsake the assembling of ourselves together, I did it anyway and withdrew from everyone. (As a side note: please always be kind to people despite their demeanor. If someone is short and snaps at you, perhaps they have a broken heart. Instead of retaliating, ask yourself if it's possible they are going through a difficult time and give them the benefit of the doubt.) I am not proud of my behavior and how I handled my grief. I don't think I seriously sought the presence of God for months after my mother passed away. Simply put, I was heartbroken and devastated. My best friend was gone, and I cried out, "Why, God, why?"

I knew there were many possible reasons as to why my mother died too soon. One was that my older sister passed away when she was in her early forties. My mother was never really the same after her death, and she lived with a lot of guilt and brokenness. I know that if she ever got a glimpse of heaven and saw my sister, she would have kissed this old world goodbye.

In my mother's last days, I know she was moving in and out of heaven, because she was sharing things that no one could possibly know. At one point, she described a wedding gown made just for her. She told about it in detail, such as the white pearls and jewels that were intricately sewn into the garment. She went on to say how all of her favorite designs were sewn in the dress, which was made just for her. I believe she was describing her wedding dress, made for her to wear when she met her long-awaited Bridegroom, Jesus. She saw many other interesting things, too. One thing she shared that puzzled me was that everyone was having fun in heaven. She described a playground for children and told me my two boys were going to love it there. Maybe we don't understand all of this, but I choose to believe that heaven is going to be a blast. Oh, the joy she must have felt to see her parents and loved ones waiting for her on the other side!

After my mother's death, the Holy Spirit helped me to see that physical death is a heavenly celebration, and as a result, my emotional healing eventually began. I drew closer to God and dared to dream again. This time was different, though. My dreaming and visions for my life took on a whole new purpose and level. I was determined to continue my mother's legacy of faith and share with others what she had taught me. God truly does turn all things for our good.

Remember that when you are in a pit, it is only for a season. Understand that it won't last forever. You *will* get out of that pit. *How?* You might ask. Start by crying out to God, confessing your sin, and speaking God's Word over your situation.

For he will deliver the needy who cry out. (Psalm 72:12 NIV)

True delivery out of the pit will take more than mere manpower. Mankind doesn't have the ability or patience, nor the strong arm to pull ourselves out of the pit. People can be there to help, but they cannot heal or deliver us. We should never expect people (not even a pastor, teacher, prophet, etc.) to be our deliverer. They are not capable of what only God can do for us. I'm not saying that God does not use people to guide us out of our pit, but ultimately it will be Jehovah Himself who delivers us from it. Looking toward people for our answer will only set us up for disappointment or failure. We must trust in a Deliverer who is with us for the long haul. The apostle Paul said it like this: He has delivered us; He will deliver us, and in Him, we trust that He will still deliver us.[27] I call this a lifetime warranty.

Be encouraged that no pit experience lasts forever. Just like the seasons in our life come and go, so will our tests and trials. God promises to never leave or forsake us. That is good news! Even when people let us down or abandon us, God will always be right by our side. When He gives us a dream to strive for and begins that good work in us, He will be faithful to complete it.[28]

If you find yourself holding a big bowl of pits, look past them and see the cherries instead. You may not always understand what God is doing behind the scenes of your life, but you can be confident that He loves you and is working for your good if you are His child. Trust Him and believe in Him, and He will help you to dream again because He came to give life and give it to you more abundantly.[29]

> *And we know that in all things God works for the good of those who love Him, who have been called according to His purpose.* (Romans 8:28 NIV)

Dream Killers

As God is working behind the scenes for our good, the enemy of our souls is working in secret for our destruction. Once a dream has been birthed into a person's heart, the enemy sends dream killers into their life. Dream killers are people who shoot down our aspirations with negativity. I have learned that when people can't see themselves fulfilling their own dreams, they certainly don't want to see anyone else fulfill their dreams, either. Dream killers don't have to be our enemies. They can be family, friends, acquaintances, or total strangers. These people start telling us everything that could go wrong and how unattainable our dreams are. Don't be too sensitive to others' opinions of your dreams. God gave your dreams to you and not to them. Some people are just unhappy people who may admire your ambition but who really do not want you or anyone else to succeed. Be on the alert.

Some dream killers believe their job is to keep us grounded in reality so that we won't get hurt. Their actions and words are an attempt to protect us from disappointment. Many of them have tried and failed in their own lives, and so they question how we could possibly succeed in our own. (Personally, I would like to ask them how many times they tried, and encourage them to try again.) When your dream begins to unfold, your success will be evident to all, and it might be the very thing they need to witness in order to spur them toward success for themselves.

Discernment is especially needed when being on guard against dream killers. It is important to note that not all negative counsel comes from dream killers. Sometimes God will put people into our lives to provide guidance for the attainment of our dreams or to protect us from harm that might come our way in the process of achieving our dreams. It is important for us not to alienate ourselves as we pursue our dreams. Some people are meant to be in our lives to foster and nurture us. When discerning, look for the fruits of that person and evidence whether they are "for" you and not just "with" you. Ask yourself: *Will they pick up the rope and help me pull, or are they watching and waiting to join only when my success looks imminent?*

We can avoid many dream killers by just being careful with whom we share our dreams. The Bible says not to cast our pearls before pigs or they will trample them under their feet, and then turn and tear us to pieces.[30] (Sounds like a dream killer to me!) Remember that when we share our dreams with others, while we may be extremely excited about the dream, not everyone else will be. Joseph can testify to this. You can always share your dreams with God, though. Ask Him to share His dreams about you, as well. His dreams will always be bigger, and He will always cheer you on.

There Is Always Hope

Despite pitfalls, dream killers, etc., we must be convinced that God is good. It doesn't matter what has happened in the past or how disappointed we have been, there is always hope for our future. God has a plan for you, and He obviously is not finished, or you wouldn't be reading this book today. Instead, you would be in heaven because your assignment here on earth would be finished.

In struggling to reach your goals and dreams, some of you are building walls around yourself and against God. You might not admit it, but it's true. Some of you are not sure that you can trust God with your life, because life hasn't turned out the way you expected. You exercised your faith, and yet things did not go your way. God knows what is best for you. Perhaps the things you are believing God for could have been the things that would have destroyed you.

Many people are experiencing dry and dead places in life. They are in desert places, where it feels like nothing is happening and all hope is dead. Things don't seem to be moving, and no refreshing water is in sight.

Even if we are dealing with spiritual, emotional, financial, or situational problems, we can still have hope in Jesus Christ. When we are in a valley of dryness, we can remember what Ezekiel did.[31] The Lord set him in the middle of a valley full of bones and asked, "Can these bones live?" Ezekiel replied, "Sovereign Lord, you alone know." Then God told Ezekiel to speak to the bones and tell to them to hear the Word of the Lord and come to life. When Ezekiel did what he was told, the bones came together, the bodies re-formed before his very eyes. Then God told him to speak breath (symbolizing "spirit") into the bodies, and when Ezekiel did, the bodies came alive.

Instead of focusing on the dry bones and giving up, Ezekiel opted to fulfill a great purpose and speak life over death. If God can take dead and dry bones and make them come to life, then He can (and will) bring life into your situation, as well. When you speak the Word of the Lord to your circumstances, God will cause life to come back to your dry valley, too. In the midst of a dead place, ask the Holy Spirit to come in and breathe life into you. Trust God that He knows what is best for you and ask Him to help you dream again. Revive your passion and joy for life. There is always hope.

****

When Joseph first had a dream, I'm sure he had no idea that he would end up in a pit or all that his future would hold. I am sure he did not always understand what God was doing in his life. On the surface, things did not look good, and Joseph's dreams certainly didn't match his circumstances. The take-home message is that the enemy may have had a plot, but God has a plan, and God's plan always prevails. The Lord will give us strength to endure our adversity if we will put our trust in Him. You probably won't understand everything, but God has a great plan for your life if you won't give up.

> *"I know the plans I have for you," declares the LORD. "Plans to prosper you and not harm you, plans to give you hope and a future."* (Jeremiah 29:11 NIV)

How has the enemy tried to trick you into giving up on your dream?

Who has God placed in your life to be a dream encourager and not a dream killer?

What does God think about you and your dream?

Nehemiah Picked Up the Pieces, and So Can You

When the Israelites were in exile, Nehemiah was the cupbearer for Artaxerxes, the king of Persia. After much weeping and mourning accompanied with fasting and praying for his people, Nehemiah's obvious distress showed on his face one day when serving the king. When the king questioned Nehemiah's sadness, he lamented for the city of Jerusalem, which lay in waste, and he requested that the king allow him to return to the city and rebuild it. The king granted Nehemiah's request, and he set out with a monumental dream.

When the surrounding Israelite enemies all heard that the walls of Jerusalem were quickly being restored, they became very angry and conspired together to attack Jerusalem and to create confusion. Nehemiah's response was to position men at the openings of the wall with their swords, spears, and bows. Half of the men worked at construction, while the other half were armed and ready for battle. Those men who built on the wall, as well as those who carried burdens, all worked with one hand, as the other hand constantly held a weapon. The trumpeter stayed by Nehemiah's side ready to rally the Israelites to battle should it come.

At one point during the rebuilding, the surrounding enemies sent Nehemiah a message to meet them in the plain of Ono to talk. Nehemiah returned the messenger with a no-thank-you and explained that he was too busy to stop his great task. (Personally, I pray we all have enough sense to decline an invitation to join our enemies at some place called "Oh no"!) The enemies didn't give up and sent messengers with the same request four more times, each one returned by Nehemiah with a refusal to meet. The fifth messenger brought a threat. Some of the Israelites began to worry about the safety of Nehemiah, and one in particular tried to persuade him to hide out in the temple. Nehemiah discerned that the man was hired from the enemies, and he refused to cower. Despite all the threats, deception, and opposition, Nehemiah led his people to rebuild the wall in only fifty-two days.

Like Nehemiah, we, too, can pick up the pieces of broken dreams and rebuild the promises that God has given us.

Get a Plan

No doubt that Nehemiah the cupbearer never dreamed how the day would end when he was preparing the king's cup that morning. That day was a *kairos* moment in Nehemiah's life—a supreme moment when his destiny met up with God's timing. The last thing Nehemiah probably expected was for the king to take an interest in the servant's heavy heart. Nevertheless, on the heels of his initial shock, Nehemiah quickly recovered and sprang into action when he realized that he had the ear of the king. Not only did Nehemiah unashamedly share his heart's desire for his homeland, but he also bravely requested permission to return and rebuild it. And not only that, Nehemiah boldly asked the king for provisions, a sign that he was already formulating a plan.

Nehemiah's request indicated that he was planning for his immediate needs as well as long-term ones. He asked for a letter from the king to guarantee his safe passage through the various regions on his journey to Jerusalem. He also requested another letter to the keeper of the forest to give him timber for the gates in the city wall and for the house he would occupy there. Nehemiah's fantastic planning continued to shine as he assessed the city walls and the repairs needed, set up defenses for the builders, and petitioned financial relief for the people.

The Bible tells us that before Nehemiah embarked on his dream, he spent day and night in prayer. It's not always enough to merely pray for our purpose, though. Like Nehemiah, we need to engage the planning gear, too.

I'm being honest when I tell you that I spent many years praying for my dreams to be fulfilled, and I made very little (and I do mean *very* little) progress in the planning department. I was frustrated all the time, and I could not understand why things simply did not fall into place. Eventually I realized that a plan was required.

After praying about a purpose, then planning for it, the next logical step would be to act on it. Oh, how many times this step trips people up! We can learn from Nehemiah here, too. He recognized the opportune time for him to act, and he stepped out in faith. Many of us jump out too quickly and miss the sidewalk, so to speak, while others appear to be sleepwalking. We must practice discernment. If we don't have peace about a situation, then we should wait on the Lord to give us the green light. If we sense a yellow light, then we need to proceed with caution, because God-ordained resources and connections may still be en route to us.

Once we get on track with our plan, we need to keep focused on what God has called us to do and ask Him daily to help us along the way. I continue to consult God on a daily basis about my purpose in life. I may not get immediate answers, but by praying continually, I know that God is involved in my destiny, and I allow Him free rein to change my course however He sees fit.

Many people talk about their dreams for their future, but they never develop a plan to fulfill them. I used to be one of those people. Now, though, I understand that people who plan for their dreams and follow through with them, will see them accomplished. Even if we do not understand what is happening in our lives, our plans will work for our good in the end. How do I know this? Because the Word of God promises that all things work together for good to those who love the Lord and are called according to His purpose.[32]

Start Small, Go Big

If anyone knew how to start small and go big, it would be Nehemiah. Although he started out as a servant in the king's service, he eventually became a governor in Judah and led the people to the rebuilding of Jerusalem. Nehemiah understood the timing for the transition from small to big. He seized the moment when he had the king's ear and asked him for three things:

1) permission to leave
2) letters
3) wood

At first glance, these may seem like small requests; however, consider that he was actually asking for the following:

> 1) Nehemiah asked to leave his job, thus abandoning a highly trusted and difficult-to-fill position, in order to rebuild a city that was considered an enemy to the king. This sort of request normally would have resulted in death.

> 2) Nehemiah asked for the king to prepare letters to the governors of the regions that he would cross on his way to Jerusalem. These letters would force the regions to grant Nehemiah, an Israelite enemy, the right to safe passage through their territories. This request could have created political tension for the king and caused uprisings in the regions.

> 3) Nehemiah asked the king to write a letter to the keeper of the king's forest, granting Nehemiah enough wood to build the gates in the city wall and also the house that he would occupy in Jerusalem. Not only did

Nehemiah ask to rebuild the city, but now he was asking the king to pay for it, too.

Despite the costs, the king granted all that Nehemiah asked, and Nehemiah didn't stop to question why. Instead, he went on with his plan and began rebuilding the city. Later, while working alongside his brethren, he noted the outcry of oppression coming from them. Nehemiah rebuked the nobles and rulers of Judah and asked them to stop the usury and restore everything to the Israelites, including their lands, houses, and also a hundredth of the taxes they had paid. Even though the request was huge, the rulers agreed to do as Nehemiah asked.

Nehemiah had the gift of faith, which helped him to start small and ask big. He also had talents such as planning, organizing, persuasion, and discernment.

God puts gifts and talents inside all of us, but it is up to us to seek Him and find out what they are. If you are unsure what gifts you have, start by doing what you know or love. For example, if you're good at working with kids, then try children's ministry or working in the nursery. Before I ever stepped up to a pulpit to speak, I spent over twelve years in children's ministry using my education degree for the kingdom of God. I know that in my own life, my gifts unfold when I obey God and exercise them. I look for opportunities, whether it be at church or in the local grocery store.

Connections are another way God equips us to fulfill our purpose. When I began to pursue radio ministry, my number of connections was small. However, in less than two years, I had the privilege to interview Nicolas Cage (lead actor) and Paul Lalonde (producer) from the movie *Left Behind*; Pastor Todd Burpo from the movie and bestselling book *Heaven Is For Real*; Andrea Logan White, the actress and producer of the movie *Mom's Night Out*; Cliff Marshall, the Cincinnati Bengals pro-football trainer; and many more.

People took note of my celebrity guests and began asking how I could possibly connect with so many prominent people that quickly. The answer was simple. First of all, I just ask. The Bible says ask and you shall receive.[33] Many people don't have because they don't ask. Second, I obeyed God and He put His hand of favor on what I was doing. He promises to bless whatever I set my hands to do.[34]

One of the keys to reaching your dream is to start small, do it with all your might, and then trust that God will increase the work of your hands.

There's No "I" in *Team*

It has been said by many great leaders that no one can row his or her boat alone and make great progress. Nehemiah was a man with a vision and a plan, but most of all, he was a team player.

Nehemiah understood the concept of a team, and no sooner did he arrive in Jerusalem than people joined him without even knowing his cause or intentions. They must have seen something in him that drew them in. Perhaps they identified with his love for Jerusalem and his grief for its demise. The best teams always share a vision and a passion for its fulfillment, and everyone on Nehemiah's team wanted the same thing he did. They stood united, and they refused to fall like the broken city wall. Although Nehemiah led the crew, he was seen as one of them, and he considered himself a servant to the goal right alongside his fellow builders.

Nehemiah was determined, and his determination was contagious. Like Nehemiah, we need to surround ourselves with people who are resolute and unyielding to failure. Their stamina will fuel our fire of commitment, and vice versa. When trouble arises (as it always does), our determination must match that of our team in order to overcome the opposition. We must not stand alone in our personal will.

Teams who work seamlessly together are ones that operate in an attitude of respect. Nehemiah valued his fellow team members and never exalted himself above them. Even when he was appointed their governor, he did not take food or money from them like other rulers did, nor did he stop working on the wall with his own hands. Instead, he carefully listened to their ideas and demonstrated their importance by caring for them. We need to heed Nehemiah's example and never exalt ourselves above other people, especially those helping us.

I am surrounded by many incredible people in my life. Every person is important, and I recognize their worth and know that their assignment of helping me is of no less significance than my own duties. When I am in the limelight, I am no more valuable than the people running the cameras or sweeping the floors. We all have roles in the Kingdom, including the fulfilment of our own divine purpose as well as our assistance in helping others fulfill theirs. While we are the leader in our own endeavors, we are also called to be the supporters in other people's efforts. Together, we lift up one other. As a side note, I believe the ministry of helps is one of the most overlooked, but important ministries in the body of Christ. Can you imagine how hard it would be to complete the tasks and organize the work of God without the help of others? People gifted in this area miraculously see and attend to every little detail that needs to be done in order to make everything run smoothly for the leaders. They are amazing!

Our utmost purpose on earth is to spread the gospel of Jesus and make disciples.[35] Through the Holy Spirit, we have gifts and talents that are not to be used to subject people to our commands, but to edify the body and accomplish our purpose. This means that fulfillment of our dreams and purposes is part of furthering the Kingdom. When we succeed, others along on our ride will, too, and likewise, when we've helped others succeed, we get to join in their successes, too. We are a team.

Nehemiah put his own dream team together, and we should, too. We must surround ourselves with people who share our vision and are determined to move forward, while always appreciating those whom God sends our way and remembering to respect them.

The Fear Factor

Fear is a strong human emotion and could very well be the number-one thing that hinders us from fulfilling our dreams. While the thought of death would paralyze almost any person, most times our fears revolve around potential failure.

Nehemiah had to overcome many fears of failure. He could have looked at his circumstances and the seemingly impossible task of rebuilding Jerusalem and given up. The situation appeared hopeless, the conditions of the city were terrible, the city walls were broken, and the gates had been burned. In addition,

Nehemiah had to face the fear of death. Not only did he ask the king for things that would normally get someone killed, he also had to deal with the Israelites' enemies during the repair of the wall.

When the Israelites' enemies heard that Nehemiah and his team were rebuilding the wall, they conspired to take Nehemiah out of commission with bodily harm during a friendly rendezvous. What was his response? He sent a message to them, basically saying that he was busy doing something incredible and couldn't meet with them. After four more requests followed by the same answer, the enemies tried a different approach. They threatened to spread rumors that Nehemiah and the Israelites planned to rebel and that was why they were rebuilding the wall. They accused him of proclaiming himself to be the king of Judah, and they threatened to report it to the king if he didn't meet with them. Such accusations would undoubtedly result in Nehemiah's death by virtue of treason. Still unshaken, Nehemiah denied the allegations, accused them of lying, and refused to meet their demands. In one last attempt to thwart Nehemiah, the enemies hired a spy among the

Israelites to try to persuade Nehemiah to flee his impending death and hide in the temple. He refused to stop his work and hide. Despite all the death threats, Nehemiah did not relinquish his purpose to fear.

We all face fear, but we have a choice in how we respond. When fear comes at us, we need to resist pushing the panic button, stay calm, and pray through it. Above all, we must always remember to seek God for the answers in the midst of our distress. Franklin Roosevelt once stated that we have nothing to fear but fear itself. Most often, the thing we fear is not what takes us out of our game—in reality, it is the fear itself that we allow to remove us.

As Joel Osteen once stated, "You can't play it safe your whole life and expect to reach your highest potential. You've got to be willing to take some risks." Without fail, we will encounter fear as we walk out our purpose and dreams in life. God will sometimes require us to step out in faith into the unknown. During these daunting times, we must be willing to displace our fears with trust in Him and reach for the stars. If we still cannot quench the fear, then, like

Joyce Meyer always says, "Do it afraid." Don't let fear keep you from reaching your destiny.

If you insist on harboring fear, then let that fear arise from the idea of standing before the Lord one day and having to explain to Him why you were too scared to do what He asked.

Nothing Is Impossible With God

Nehemiah knew that the future of Jerusalem was worth the effort, even though the task seemed impossible. He understood that with God, all things are possible.

When I graduated from college and began my career as a teacher, I started seriously considering the prospect of a husband. Whereas many people meet their spouses at their workplace, this did not seem like a plausible option for me since I worked at an elementary school surrounded by other women and children. I told my sister, Terri, that it would be a miracle for me to find a husband there.

One day, a group of salespeople offering employment benefits came to our school to enroll us. In that group was a good-looking man who caught my eye. The next year when they returned, he and I began to date. We married six months later and are still happily married today with two incredible sons. What I thought was impossible, God made possible.

Throughout the years, God has continued to show me that nothing is too hard for Him. Nevertheless, when God first spoke to my heart about having a radio show, my first reaction was "Are You kidding me?" The task seemed impossibly impossible. I questioned the voice I heard and almost resigned that it was my imagination playing tricks on me. Despite my fears and doubts, I made a choice right then—even if in my mind there was a small chance that it was God, I would be obedient anyway.

What impossible task has God called you to do? Are you still questioning yourself and God? You are more than what you think, and with God, you can do more than you could ever fathom. We are called to shake the nations for Christ. It starts with us stepping out in our own cities and spheres of influence. Make the decision that you are going to remain sold out for God no matter how hard the task may seem.

Dreams NEVER Expire

You might as well go ahead and tear up the blueprints you have for your life, because God's ways are higher than your ways and His thoughts are higher than your thoughts.[36] I really believe that if the task seems possible and easy, then you probably aren't thinking big enough.

Squirrel!!

When the Israelite enemies heard that the walls of Jerusalem were being restored, they became angry, and they conspired together to attack the people and create confusion. Our enemy does the same thing to us. The greatest weapon for his assault is distraction.

Anyone who has seen the Disney movie *Up* remembers the dog who was so easily distracted with the possibility of a squirrel being nearby. In reality, most of us have things in our lives that immediately turn our full attention. A distraction takes our attention away from what we are supposed to be doing. According to the *Merriam-Webster Dictionary*,[37] distraction occurs as a result of something that makes it difficult for you to think or pay attention, something that amuses or entertains you so that you do not want to complete your task, or something that causes you to be very annoyed or upset and unable to focus.

If we belong to Christ, then satan can't destroy us but he can hinder us. He uses distractions to weaken our faith and wear us down.

Distractions come in many various forms, and we must be constantly aware of them. It is important to know that simple distractions are just as dangerous as complex ones. Oftentimes, the enemy hits us with something minimal and then works to turn it into a stronghold (i.e., a belief or issue that negatively controls or influences our life). For example, a slight crush on someone who does not share your beliefs can lead to a relationship that pulls you away from God and your destiny.

Not all distractions come from ungodly people, but some arise from Christians with good intentions. One day after one of my radio broadcasts, a Christian lady minister asked me to stop teaching about false hope. She felt that it was deceiving to give people hope amidst impossible situations, such as incurable illnesses. Her comments caught me by surprise, especially considering that she was a minister and would presumably know the Word of God concerning healing. I averted any further distraction by sending her all the scripture references I used to teach healing on my broadcast. The Bible also speaks of this sort of distraction and cautions us about who we come into agreement with because they could distract us from our service.[38]

Probably the biggest distractions today are electronic devices. People have become obsessed with checking their email, text messages, and social media posts every few minutes, making it difficult to focus for long periods of time. In addition, posts on social media trigger emotional distractions for people who read about other folks' successes while they, themselves, are struggling.

Addiction is another type of distraction. If the enemy has a person consumed with finding the next drink, then they obviously won't be looking for ways to fulfill their destiny. If your distraction is an addiction, then you have a serious problem and need to ask someone to help you escape it.

In order to deal with distractions, we need to divert the oncoming ones and eradicate the existing ones.

We must stay fixed on our assignment. The enemy is a master at keeping us distracted with busyness so that we forget our main focus. I know in my personal life that whenever I make a determined decision to do something (such as work on my next book), my phone calls almost triple on the day I set aside for the task.

Have you ever started your day with lots of great ideas, goals, and plans, only to find that there were so many distractions that very little was accomplished? Disciplining ourselves is critical if we want to complete our God-given tasks in His prescribed timing. Each morning, list your daily goals and be determined to see them through. At the end of the day, ask yourself whether you accomplished all that you wanted to do for the Kingdom of God that day and make a plan to cover anything you missed.

There are so many opportunities to be distracted that if we are not disciplined in our thinking, we will never stay on course, or it will take us twice the amount of time to complete a task. We only get one chance at this thing called life, and I don't know about you, but I don't have time for distractions.

Dreams NEVER Expire

Keep On Keeping On

Despite the distractions, regardless of the usury, and in the face of death threats, Nehemiah stayed his course and finished the seemingly impossible task of rebuilding the wall in just fifty-two days. It is one thing to start a task, but quite another to finish it. The only difference between a successful person and an unsuccessful person is that one of them did not give up.

We are all assaulted with doubts, fears, and insecurities about ourselves. However, truly successful people plow through these things anyway and drive toward their finish line. You can still get to your finish line, too. You only have to take one step at a time.

Step one is to stop making excuses as to why you aren't qualified. God did not say that He calls the equipped; He said that He equips the called.[39] Consider the following great biblical people and how God saw fit to do great things through them despite their issues. If they can do it, you can, too, if you just don't give up!

Abraham was old.[40]

Jeremiah and Timothy were young.[41]
Jacob was a liar.[42]
Leah was considered ugly.[43]
Joseph was abused.[44]
Moses had a speech impediment.[45]
Gideon was afraid.[46]
David was an adulterer and a murderer.[47]
Samson was a womanizer.[48]
Rahab was a prostitute.[49]
Elijah was suicidal.[50]
Jonah ran from God.[51]
Naomi's sons and husband were dead.[52]
Job went bankrupt.[53]
Peter denied Christ three times.[54]
Martha worried about everything.[55]
Mary Magdalene was cleansed of seven demons.[56]
The Samaritan woman at the well had five husbands.[57]
And best of all...
Lazarus was dead![58]

Step two is to encourage yourself, even if others won't, and refuse to allow what others think about you to become your future. Renew your mind daily with scriptures that inspire you to strive for your dream.

** You are a child of the King.[59]
** You can do all things through Christ, who strengthens you.[60]

- ** You are God's workmanship, created in Christ for good works.[61]
- ** You are more than a conqueror through Christ.[62]
- ** There is no condemnation for you because you are in Christ Jesus.[63]
- ** You will fight a good fight, you will finish your course, and you will keep the faith.[64]
- ** God has not given you a spirit of fear, but of power, love, and a sound mind.[65]
- ** With God nothing is impossible, and all things are possible.[66]
- ** God will count you worthy of your calling and fulfill all the good pleasure of His goodness and the work of faith with power in your life.[67]

For Step 3 and so on, just put one foot in front of the other and keep on keeping on. If the step is too large, then break it up into multiple smaller steps. Don't feel guilty for only taking small steps from time to time. They add up, and the important thing is to keep moving forward and persevere.

****

Nehemiah's dream literally lay in pieces. Nevertheless, he picked up what he had and set out to build something great.

Have your dreams been shattered? Fear not! There is hope! When we pick up the shards of our broken dreams and persevere despite the distractions, everyone will see and hear of our success and will know that nothing is impossible with God.

Dream Again

On what broken dreams have you given up?
What aspects of your dream seem impossible?
What has God already given you for your success?

Live Your Dream

Just like Joseph, we are designed by God to dream. Without a dream, we will drift aimlessly through life with no plan or purpose, whereas with a dream, we will be fulfilled and fruitful because God's nature is in us.

What dream has the Lord given you? If you have received Jesus Christ as your personal Savior, then you have a right to have your dream fulfilled by God. As a Christian, it is your responsibility to set goals and incorporate them into your life. Only then will you see the mighty hand of God upon all that you do. If you don't have a specific goal, then get one. You have to start somewhere.

Your Heart's Desire

God places dreams in our hearts, so therefore, it is His will for the dreams to come to pass.

> *Delight thyself also in the LORD and He will give thee the desires of thine heart.* (Psalm 37:4 KJV)

The only stipulation God asks is that we delight in Him first. Instead of seeking the desire to be fulfilled, seek Him, and then these desires will come to pass. God doesn't place desires and dreams in our hearts to frustrate, tease, or tempt us. He actually places them there to give us purpose and passion for life to see the dreams fulfilled.

God would not place a dream in our heart and then not want us to fulfill it. That would be cruel. God delights in seeing our purpose achieved. Everyone is created by God with an appetite to dream and a hunger to fulfill the purpose attached to it. It is the devil who sows doubt and unbelief in our minds and makes us believe God is never going to fulfill His promises. Understand this—the enemy knows that when you accomplish your God-given dreams and purposes, you are a threat to his kingdom of darkness.

Psalm 20:4 says that God gives us the desires of our hearts and makes all our plans succeed. Again, not only does God give us desires, but He also wants us to succeed in the planning of those desires. Go ahead and dream big because God (who is on your side) is a big dreamer, too. We can trust the Holy Spirit to help us get to our destiny. Psalm 32:8 (KJV) says: *"I will instruct you and teach you in the way you should go; I will counsel you with my loving eye on you."* I particularly love the way the *New Living Translation* says it: The Lord says, *"I will guide you along the best pathway for your life. I will advise you and watch over you."* Isn't that good news for us? As we begin to take the steps of faith to fulfill our dreams, God's Word vows to lead, love, guide, direct, and counsel us to the best pathway for our lives.

Start today and focus on your heart's desires. Ask God to reveal and awaken the dreams in you that maybe have been forgotten. It is never too late to dream.

See It Happen

How badly do you want to see your dream fulfilled? All of us have similar excuses as to why we can't move forward, but I dare to believe that whatever obstacles we see as holding us back, someone has succeeded with even bigger hindrances to overcome. It is not about the impediments as much as it is about the vision and the tenacity not to give up and to see it through. Success is mainly defined by those who push through the obstacles to the dream, just like Joseph. Abraham had many excuses as to why it would be impossible to birth the promised child and eventually become the father of many nations. But he believed against all odds, and so can you. It may not be the most talented, most intelligent, best-looking, or any other human attribute that guarantees success. It's those who pick up the torch and run with it until they see the end results. Keep focused on the prize of your dream coming true. Keep the picture in your mind and see it with the eye of faith.

I remember the first time I really applied this faith principle. I was about eighteen years old and in desperate need of a car. I was attending Eastern Kentucky University in Richmond, Kentucky, and needed transportation to drive back and forth to school. Our family had very little money at that time, so I prayed and asked God to provide me with a vehicle without having any clue how He would do it. I first began speaking about it to my friends. Their initial response was as bad as Joseph's brothers. In addition, they assumed I would have a car within a week or so. They began making fun of me, and when weeks and even months passed, they would say things like, "Hey, Beth, when's that car coming?" I would just say that I didn't know, and they would laugh. Nevertheless, I still kept professing it. I told everyone I knew that I was getting a car. I remember sitting on the front porch and I would picture a car driving up the driveway with me as the driver. I would see with the eye of faith and would visualize cars of all colors, sizes, and ages.

An increase of revenue flowed through my dad's business one day. Shortly thereafter, I was sitting on my front porch and my dad drove up our driveway with a new green Monte Carlo, which had a sunroof! Do you know what I did? I got in that car, thanking God all the while, drove past every friend who mocked me, and gave them a great big Princess Diana wave. While I don't recommend the I-told-you-so approach (especially the princess wave), I do recommend that you thank God when the blessing comes.

Dreams NEVER Expire

My new green Monte Carlo with a sunroof.

Speak to your dream and see it in faith. I would like to say that the car came within a few months of my first proclamation, but it was closer to a year before I saw it with my physical eyes. I didn't let the delay deter me. I never quit confessing, and I never stopped looking for it.

Put It on Paper

When God gives us a revelation about something, He has instructed us to record it.[68] One of the things I do is to keep a journal, which I use to project my goals for the next three years. Now don't panic. You may be thinking that you don't even have a goal for this week, let alone for three years.

What I am actually talking about are dream goals. These are dreams that seem outlandishly crazy to accomplish. I write my dreams and paste cut-out pictures next to them in my journal. This way I can read the dream and get a visual of it at the same time. There is just something about seeing the pictures that makes the dream get down into my spirit. It is like my car story—I had to see it first before it could come to pass.

Let me give you an example. Let's say that you have a dream to visit Hawaii. Find all sorts of pictures of the places you would like to visit there. Paste those pictures next to your written words in your journal. Try not to think about the money or how it could possibly happen. Go ahead and just dream big. Refer back to your journal entry often to reignite your passion.

Use this technique with as many dreams as you can imagine. We serve a big God who has designed us to dream and think big. I have personally witnessed that people who use this process see many of their dreams come to pass within a short period of time. It works.

Put It into Prayer and Proclamation

There are different tools we need in order to fulfill our dreams. Prayer is the most powerful one.

Prayer is actually a continual communication with our heavenly Father whereby we upload our cares, worship, and petitions and download heavenly instruction and encouragement. It is both a dialogue and a relationship with God that has the power to change our hearts and circumstances. When we earnestly pray, we enter the presence of almighty God and are inviting Him to enter our situations and accomplish His will with His power and wisdom. Prayer should be as natural as breathing and a regular part of our everyday life. When a situation arises, our first response should be to pray.

Your future success will depend on your prayer life. As you begin progressing toward Kingdom purposes, you will encounter the enemy, who wants to shut you down, discourage you, and pressure you to give up. Prayer will help bring about your victory. I once heard someone say that prayer is more powerful than an atomic bomb. The prayer of faith will move your mountains and bury your enemy under them.

Proclamation is another powerful instrument in our heavenly toolkit. The Bible says that the power of life and death is in our tongues.[69] We know this is especially true for our eternal life: when we confess (proclaim) Jesus is Lord with our mouth and believe in our heart, then we are saved.[70] Our words can bring death into our lives also. When we say that we don't believe our dream will ever be fulfilled, we are really saying that we don't believe God will do what He promised in His Word. Such a confession is a faith destroyer.

Here is what works for me: Find the scripture that pertains to your situation or dream, and declare that scripture every time you begin to doubt. That scripture will eventually become such a part of your belief system that you will eventually attain what you confess because your faith is at work.

Get rid of all negative speaking and begin today to proclaim what God says about your promises. When you make a decision to confess only God's Word and promises, you will see your promises come to pass and watch your doubt and fears vanish.

Fear and doubt must go as you speak God's Word. Watch faith begin to dominate as you change your confessions and begin to proclaim truth over your promises.

Put Your Hands to Work

Things do not normally just fall into our lap. Deuteronomy 28:8 says that *"The LORD will send a blessing on your barns and on everything you put your hands to. The Lord God will bless you in the land he is giving you"* (NIV).

Notice the scripture says that you have to do something. You have to put your hands to work and thereby, give God something to work with. Nehemiah understood this and labored with both his mouth and his hands. You may find yourself getting additional education and training, as well as making new connections with people.

A couple of years ago, I was at a point in my life when I had successfully taught classes at my church and written many articles for a magazine; however, something kept telling me on the inside that there was more that God wanted me to do. One day I was out jogging and crying out to God about which direction I should take for my life. As I was jogging around Lunken Airport in Cincinnati, I noticed a billboard for a local Christian radio station. A still, small voice told me to call and inquire about a radio spot. (As a note, I never expected my sign from God to literally come in the form of a billboard.)

Right here is where many people miss God-given opportunities. They immediately start talking negative and defeat themselves before they even take a step. We all deal with the second voice from the enemy designed to cancel the first voice from God. We have to ignore it and decide that we are going to at least look into what God might be saying to us.

I decided to follow through, realizing that I didn't have anything to lose by at least checking into the station, and I'm so glad I did. I instantly had favor with the station manager. He offered me a prime-time spot and a great deal so that I could at least try it out. My husband and I prayed about it and knew that speaking the Word of God over the airways could never be a bad thing.

To make a long story short, after just twelve months, our broadcasts reached over thirty-three nations and forty states. Several months after the initial broadcast, the Lord finally gave me the name "Triumphant Living" for the program. It was a reminder to me of how most of us want the whole picture of what to do before we step out and do anything. That's not faith, though. Faith is believing what you can't see and not expecting to always understand what God is doing through us.

The main goal with the broadcast is to teach people how to live triumphantly in Christ Jesus through the Word of God. With the help of technology and the Internet, our program is able to play in orphanages in Africa, in crusades in India, and in many other places, including third-world countries.

When I first started, I was not sure where it was all going and I did not know whether anyone would listen. I just applied the Word of God, which promised me that anything I set my hands to do, God would bless.

Beth Stewart

Dream Again

What desires has God given you?

What scriptures will you confess and proclaim over your dreams?

What kinds of things do you need to put your hands to work doing in order to achieve your dream?

Dreams NEVER Expire

You Can Do It!

You will almost never see the whole picture when you start out with the vision for your future. It may even look like it's not going anywhere and get hard sometimes. But if you don't give up, God's Word will come to pass, and the thing you started will succeed.

I often ponder what would have happened had I seen the billboard as just a sign instead of a sign from God or What if I had given up on the radio broadcast idea and thought it was too hard. I felt unqualified, as I had no media knowledge, radio experience, or formal degree in broadcasting. I remember being a nervous wreck when walking into the broadcast station. The radio manager asked me whether I had any experience in radio, and I nervously said no. As we spoke further, I shared my heart and explained that God had directed me to do this. I am not sure what he thought, but he gave me the encouragement I needed and helped me along the way.

In the beginning, I talked so fast (because of my nerves) that listeners could barely understand me. In fact, one listener called in and said, "Slow down, sister." I say all of this to tell you that it's okay to be scared and apprehensive when embarking on something new. The key is to know down deep that you are doing what God has called you to do and to just press on despite the fear. Eventually the fear will leave, and you will have the victory over the enemy's attempts to thwart your destiny. I simply listened to the still, small voice that told me to call a radio station and inquire about it, and God took it from there. If I can do it, you can, too!

Stay focused and don't give up. Perseverance and patience is all you need to see your dream come to pass. Surround yourself with positive people who will encourage you. Forget past mistakes and dare to believe again. If God said it, then it will happen if you don't give up. You can do it. Remember the trials of Abraham, Joseph, Nehemiah, and many other people in the Bible, and how they overcame adversity and obstacles. If they overcame, then you can, too.

What are you waiting for? Start dreaming again and work toward your goals. Get moving in the direction of your ambitions and watch the mighty hand of God work on your behalf. It's never too late. Dreams NEVER expire!!!

Dreams NEVER Expire

ABOUT THE AUTHOR

Beth Stewart realized the call on her life when she made a commitment for Christ at the age of seventeen. Her passion is to set the captives free through the truth of Jesus Christ and God's Word.

Beth is the founder of *Triumphant Living* radio ministry and the CEO of Beth Stewart Ministries, which reaches over thirty nations. A Bible teacher, author, public speaker, and radio talk host, Beth also holds a BA in education, an MA in education, and a BS in theology. She speaks to many church groups, conferences, businesses, and organizations in the effort to bring hope and encouragement to help facilitate the fulfillment of destiny and God-given dreams within people.

ABOUT BETH STEWART MINISTRIES

Beth Stewart Ministries was birthed with a passion to reach a lost and dying world. Our primary goal is to win the lost to Jesus Christ to ensure their salvation. Our mission is to reach around the world to bring the good news of Jesus Christ to as many souls as possible. We are doing this through speaking, books, street ministry, and radio broadcasts.

BethStewartMinistries.com

Beth Stewart Ministries is a 501(c)(3) nonprofit organization. All donations are tax-deductible.

Donate via PayPal at info@BethStewartMinistries.com or mail your donation to Beth Stewart Ministries, 525 West 5th Street Suite 334, Covington, KY 41011.

Author's Acknowledgments

I would like to acknowledge my loving mother, who is now in her heavenly mansion, for showing me the love of Jesus Christ with her faithfulness and love. Without her prayers, I honestly don't know where my life would have gone.

I would also like to thank the following people, because without their help, this book would still be a dream:

WC Stewart

Alex and Austin Stewart

Darlene Bishop

Terri Meredith

Heather May

April Collins

Hope Keltner

Jennifer Minigh

REVIEW REQUEST

I hope you have gained some helpful knowledge from *Dreams NEVER Expire*.

Now that you've read this book, if you enjoyed it, then please let other readers know. Let's share the knowledge and help people fulfill their God-given destinies and fulfill their God-given dreams. Let's encourage one another to be all God has made us to be. After all, we are all in this walk of life together.

Dreams NEVER Expire

SCRIPTURES AND REFERENCES

[1] Genesis 13:6, 15:1-6; 17:6-8; 18:10
[2] Numbers 23:19 NIV
[3] Genesis 12:1-3
[4] Genesis 16:1-4
[5] Genesis 15:4-5
[6] Genesis 17:17
[7] Genesis 18:12
[8] Genesis 16:2-3
[9] Genesis 15:2-3 NLT
[10] Ephesians 1:4
[11] Jeremiah 1:5
[12] Romans 11:29
[13] Matthew 25:14-30
[14] Deuteronomy 31:6 NKJV
[15] Romans 8:28
[16] Genesis 17:1-2
[17] Genesis 26:5
[18] Romans 11:6
[19] James 1:5
[20] John 10:10
[21] Deuteronomy 2:7
[22] Deuteronomy 28:8
[23] Genesis 37:27-28
[24] Genesis 37:5-7
[25] Genesis 37:9
[26] Isaiah 59:19; John 10:10
[27] 2 Corinthians 1:10
[28] Philippians 1:6
[29] John 10:10
[30] Matthew 7:6
[31] Ezekiel 37: 1-10
[32] Romans 8:28
[33] Mark 11:24
[34] Deuteronomy 28:8
[35] Matthew 28:18
[36] Isaiah 55:8-9
[37] distraction. 2014. In Merriam-Webster.com. Retrieved September 23, 2014, from http://www.merriam-webster.com/dictionary/distraction
[38] 1 Corinthians 7:35
[39] Hebrews 13:21
[40] Genesis 17
[41] Jeremiah 1:6-7; 2 Timothy 1:2
[42] Genesis 27:19
[43] Genesis 29:17
[44] Genesis 37:24-36
[45] Exodus 4:10
[46] Judges 6:21-23
[47] 2 Samuel 11:3-27
[48] Judges 14
[49] Joshua 2:1
[50] 1 King 19
[51] The book of Jonah
[52] Ruth 1:3
[53] The book of Job
[54] Matthew 26:69-70

Dreams NEVER Expire

---

[55] Luke 10:40
[56] Mark 16:9
[57] John 4:18
[58] John 11
[59] Romans 8:17
[60] Philippians 4:13
[61] Ephesians 2:10
[62] Romans 8:37
[63] Romans 8:1
[64] 2 Timothy 4:7
[65] 2 Timothy 1:7 KJV
[66] Luke 1:37; Matthew 19:26
[67] 2 Thessalonians 1:11
[68] Habakkuk 2:2
[69] Proverbs 18:21
[70] Romans 10:9

www.ingramcontent.com/pod-product-compliance
Lightning Source LLC
Chambersburg PA
CBHW051954290426
44110CB00015B/2242